FAITHFUL
in Small Things

HOW GOD GREW A MINISTRY FROM ONE HOME TO SERVE 104 NATIONS

JOETH STRICKLAND

Faithful in Small Things:

How God Grew a Ministry
from One Home to Serve 104 Nations

Joeth Strickland

BIBLE SCRIPTURES

Printed in the United States of America

⅋ SPIRIT MEDIA
www.spiritmedia.us
1249 Kildaire Farm Rd STE 112
Cary, NC 27511
1 (888) 800-3744

Books › Self-Help › Relationships › Interpersonal Relations

Paperback ISBN: 978-1-961614-48-2
Hardback ISBN: 978-1-961614-49-9
Audiobook ISBN: 978-1-961614-50-5
eBook ISBN: 978-1-961614-47-5
Library of Congress Control Number: 2023916680

TABLE OF CONTENTS

How God Prepared For and Grew This Ministry

What We Do And Why

DEDICATION

I dedicate this book to the love of my life, my husband, James Ashley Strickland Jr., now with our Lord.

He was my pen pal prayer partner when we were just teenagers. Our first shared service to the Lord was on a bus route for our church. From then on, we were co-laborers for 42 years. He worked full-time to support our family, so we could raise our children in a Christian home. Because of his hard work, I was able to begin this ministry; the Lord grew it into what it is today.

His care through my nineteen surgeries was exceptional. Most marriages fail in these kinds of crises; ours grew stronger. He was my biggest supporter and encourager in all aspects of my life.

He was always God's servant through our family, our church, and beyond. I look forward to seeing him again in the Lord's presence.

I am so grateful my parents raised me in a Christian home and imparted to me their love for and commitment to sharing God's truth through all the world. Their faithful example and instruction made me the person I am.

INTRODUCTION

In early 2022, the whole world was focused on the war between Russia and Ukraine. At Crossing All Borders Ministries, we focused the best way we knew: by finding out what Christian missionaries and other ministry leaders in Ukraine would need and packing up shipments of donated goods for them.

The Lord led us to meet Andriy Ivenets, a Ukrainian pastor just three hours from us in Greensboro, NC. Together we started working on filling shipping containers with everyday supplies, medical, and military items that were needed. Laura Reavis, a friend from Nebraska with a medical background, suggested we put our medical supplies together into trauma kits for the front line. She contacted a doctor she knew to get a list of what would be needed. So we started filling gallon Ziploc bags with emergency medical basics—bandages, antibiotics, wound-sealing glue, and whatever else we had in our warehouse or could get people to send us.

You probably remember from the beginning of the war that one thing they really needed was tourniquets. Tourniquets stop catastrophic bleeding and can save lives. Because of that, all the tourniquets in all the markets all over the world were snapped up right off. You couldn't get tourniquets anywhere.

"Is there anything that could substitute for a tourniquet?" we wondered.

And Laura's doctor friend told us: "If you can't send tourniquets, just send a men's necktie."

Now I've gotta tell you: we've learned, over the years, that the best way to get people exactly what they need is to let God supply, and sometimes God supplies in really unexpected ways. This was one of those times.

Phone in hand, I looked up toward the warehouse ceiling. There's a crawl space up there where we put things when we have absolutely no idea what to do with them and just want to get them out of our way. Pallets full of stuff. Some things can sit there for years. And I said, still looking upward, "OK, God, that's why you sent me thirteen pallets of neckties three years ago."

The tourniquet neckties that we sent to Ukraine had Bible verses, the name Jehovah, and all kinds of Christian things on them. Some had things like "US Army," the US flag, and tanks. I've heard that the supply station in Ukraine has a US flag hanging up; they're so grateful for the aid that has come from the US. When we started running low on some supplies for the kits, they told us to just send whatever we had. Assembling the kits in Ukraine to match what the Ukrainian military issues was a way they could give some of the refugees and others something to do.

In almost forty years of collecting and shipping donated goods, God has taught me that His plans are better than mine. He knows how those donations are going to be used. He knows how we'll get them into countries where bribery and corruption block useful shipments from getting to people who need them. He knows what volunteers we need and how they can work together.

And He also taught me that the journey He planned for my life is better than I could ever have imagined. Better than I would have chosen if He'd given me the choice.

I'd never have thought that a girl who couldn't read 'til fourth grade could grow up to read and understand the detailed rules for international shipping—different for every country—and organize deliveries as large as full-sized shipping containers. I never would have guessed that my kids and I would survive a crash with a tractor-trailer, much less that the baby I was carrying then would be born healthy. I could never imagine that I'd be traveling internationally to help missions teams decide what they wanted me to send them from the generous donors who fill the ministry's warehouse. And I certainly wouldn't have thought I could do all that as a woman with disabilities who's had nineteen surgeries after that accident with the tractor-trailer.

Crossing All Borders Ministries started out almost forty years ago, when I kept just a few boxes full of donations in my breezeway. Now, God has given us a 17,000 square foot warehouse, and our all-volunteer team has shipped essential hard goods to Christian workers in 104 countries.

I tell you all that just to let you know that the best journey for anyone is the journey God has picked out for you. "For I know the plans I have for you," declares the Lord, "plans to prosper you and not to harm you, plans to give you hope and a future" Jer. 29:11 (NIV). God has made each one of us unique, and your journey is the journey God planned for you alone. This book tells about my journey. I hope it encourages you to ask God to help you understand the journey you're on with God—the journey God has given you!

HOW GOD PREPARED FOR AND GREW THIS MINISTRY

Growing Up Through Adversity

I was born in 1964 in Chapel Hill, North Carolina, pigeon-toed and with what some people call a "lazy eye." My left eye was so turned in that you mostly just saw the white. You could barely see that it was brown. At that time, my dad was studying to become an orthodontist. Little did I know how God would use the adversities in my life to give me the will to get through other difficulties I would face later in life.

My Uncle Bill was an orthodontic professor in Chapel Hill. The two had decided when Dad finished his orthodontic training they would set up a practice in Raleigh. But the war in Vietnam was heating up, and people knew there might be a military draft. So, it was recommended to him that he should sign up for the military before he started his practice because then they would have him serve in his field of specialty as a dentist. And so he signed up, which also meant we would definitely go to a foreign country.

We expected to go to Germany, which would be cool because that's where my family comes from. My maiden name is Pannkuk. If you see that name anywhere in the United States, we're all the same family. Because Dad knew the original spelling of our last name, he was excited and hoping he would get to study and find family members.

But God had other plans, and our orders were changed. They sent us to Japan.

My family moved to Japan when I was two, and we lived on a military base there. I remember my childhood in Japan so vividly. We lived at Johnson Family Housing Annex which was a US Air Force installation. It's now called Iruma Air Base, and it's home to the Japan Air Defense Force, but at that time it was a US military base. The military housing was in a circle, and our playground was at the center.

I had my first two surgeries to correct that lazy eye while we lived in Japan. The hospital was like a ward. My family said there were four beds on each side of the room, but I couldn't see anything because they had to cover my eyes after the surgery.

Saved in Japan by US Missionaries

Now, I'm going to tell you something about my family that you might find hard to believe. My parents grew up in Laurens, Iowa, and they had never even heard the plan of salvation growing up. After they married, they were living in Chapel Hill, North Carolina, and nobody ever impacted them with the Gospel there, either.

The first time they were presented the Gospel was by a neighbor while they were living in Texas. At the time, they did not understand and felt they were just fine. Trust me—that is still going on today. There are people in our community that have not been impacted with Christ. And we're thinking, "Well, everybody's got a Bible." Well, no, they don't.

So, amazingly, my parents had never understood the Gospel of Jesus Christ until we lived in Japan. They had only heard it once and they did not have any understanding of who Jesus was or any understanding of the Bible.

But there in Japan, there were these missionaries. Believe it or not, one of their sending churches was about an hour down the road from where we lived in North Carolina, but God took us all the way to Japan for us to meet them. Those missionary families impacted and changed the direction of my family and our lives.

One of the missionaries would meet with my dad every Tuesday. They played handball, and he built a relationship with my dad. You're going to hear that word relationship a lot from me because relationships are important.

Our entire salvation is built on having a personal relationship with Jesus Christ. That is what differentiates our beliefs, according to the Scriptures, from all other religions in the world. We are not in a religion; we are in a relationship. So if you do not have a good strong relationship with Christ, I urge you to pray over that.

So that missionary did that for two years . . . two years! He didn't just go hang a flier on the doorknob. He built a relationship and waited for the right time to speak so he could introduce my father to Jesus the same way he'd introduce a good friend to any other important friend of his.

Dad didn't want to come to church. "Let me just go on my way," he said. And still, the missionary played handball with him and worked with him for two years.

At that particular time, one of the missionary women would get the military wives together with the Japanese women. She would pair them up so the Japanese women could help the military wives adjust to living in Japan. There are things you need to learn when you move to another country—how to shop, how to get at least some of the foods you're used to, how to cook and do things differently. So one week they'd cook Japanese food and one week they'd cook American food.

And then, when they would sit down at the table to eat, she'd stand at the head of the table and she'd open up the Scriptures. And while she was doing that another family would come and they'd take all the kids upstairs for something called a Five-Day Club. Have you heard of those? They're held by Child Evangelism Fellowship, and that's something you can get your church involved in. Those are going on all over our country every summer.

So, my mother and my father came to know Christ first. After my mother came to know Christ, then I came to know Christ. So the impact of missions is huge in my life. I came to Christ as a four year old. I still remember it to this day. These missionaries went to Japan thinking that they were going to help lead Japanese people to Christ. But they also had a very strong presence on the military base and they had a strong influence on the military, too.

We came back to the States in 1969, and we settled at a good local church. It was just one little tiny building then. And that's where I was raised.

My parents came back with a fire for missions because of how missions impacted their lives. They were so grateful for their path. They got very involved in missions after we returned to the United States back in the '70s and '80s. Those of you that are old enough know that back then, missionaries didn't fly back and forth to visit the way they do now. We didn't have cell phones or Skype to chat with them. Missionaries would serve on the field for five years and then come home for a year of furlough.

It's pretty tough to find a place to live for 12 months when you're coming in with just a suitcase and the clothes on your back.

On a mission furlough you return to the US and have to find a place to live. My parents were able to help one missionary family, the Herseys, find a furnished place to live, and locate clothing. Mom also taught their daughter how to sew and then sent a sewing machine back with her. While in the military her contact with military wives also enabled her to find clothing that they donated to the missionary wives before they left for furlough.

My mother would work with the wives during their stay. She'd say, "What do you need that is expensive in your country? What do you need to take back for your family?"

Trust me, what's expensive is different in every country. One of the things Mom often helped with was their children's clothing. My mother was a seamstress, so she'd buy fabric and patterns and send them back with some nice little outfits.

So, I say my training for the ministry I have today started when God gave me the opportunity to help my mother help those missionaries get what they needed.

From Disability to Disability

As you may remember, it resulted in two surgeries to attempt to correct my lazy eye. That eye was so bad that I was legally blind on that side. When we came back to the States, my parents not only did a lot with world missions but also engaged with people with disabilities and less fortunate.

Our family was on a waiting list to get into a small Christian school. My first year of schooling was at a small Episcopalian school near to the rental home we lived in for a year. My parents then bought a home and moved to Cary, where I attended public school for the first year. The next year, all four of us got into the Christian school.

I really struggled to learn in school, and none of the teachers recognized the problem. I couldn't seem to learn. In first grade, my teacher just let me do artwork all day long. That was fine with me because Mom had me taking art lessons, too. She sent me to a place called the Palette Gallery, where they had me do a lot with the color red to help stimulate my eyes. I loved it because I got to stay up late with the adults for those classes!

But Mom didn't realize until the end of the year that I'd been pulled out of classes and hadn't had any first-grade education at all. None of the teachers suggested that maybe I should have been at the school for the blind since I couldn't see. The following year, we got into a private Christian school, a tiny new K-12 school that had started in South Raleigh with just one brick building. There were a little over 100 students at the time, so class sizes were really small. This small class size helped with my learning tremendously. Mom told them that I didn't know how to read yet, so maybe I should stay in first grade. And they said, "Oh, her dad's a doctor. She'll do fine."

My second grade teacher wasn't so sure and got very frustrated with me. To be fair, it was her first year out of college. I finished that year, and when I went into third grade I still didn't know how to read.

In third grade, my teacher was a lady named Edna Buffalo. She retired from teaching in public schools and then came to teach at our Christian school. She spent all of her paycheck buying things for the school. That ended up being a very good thing for me.

There were two of us in our third grade classroom who were unable to read. Mrs. Buffalo said, "You're not going out of my class until you can read on the fourth grade level with confidence." She ordered special instructional materials in large bold print that was easier for me to see to help achieve her mission.

Now, I was still wearing a patch on one eye, and I wore that eye patch until I was age twelve. When I was coming along, the main way they treated "lazy eye" was to cover the good eye and force the bad eye to do all the work of seeing. There's a certain window of time for the bad eye to get better, and so you have to do this when you're a kid.

My mom would explain this to my classroom at the beginning of every school year what the eyepatch was for. She'd bring in a lot of eyepatches and have the kids draw pictures on them. Then she'd tell them: "Look at her every day to see if she's wearing your picture. If she takes that eyepatch off, it undoes two days' work." She made them my helpers so I wouldn't get picked on.

However, that didn't stop kids from picking on me because I was pigeon-toed and had to wear special shoes. They were these saddle oxford shoes that were very expensive and very ugly. I wasn't able to wear what everyone else was wearing. Eventually, a doctor said that my feet turned in because my hip was aligned wrong, so wearing different shoes wouldn't make any difference. I was thankful for that doctor because I finally got to start buying shoes like everyone else.

By the time I was fourteen, the eye patch had done its work. I could see. I'd learned to read. I got to wear shoes just like everyone else. I thought I was through with all that hard stuff.

Birth of a Ministry: When God Can Trust You in the Small Things

So, I'm going to tell you a little bit of the background so you know where the passion comes from for serving the Lord.

When my husband Ashley and I got married, I was told that I would not be able to have children. We said, well, whether we adopt children or have them ourselves, we want to be able to teach our children. My husband and I wanted to be able to teach our children the same desire to help missionaries that we both had. So, when we first got married, we started going to a solid Bible-believing church located near where we lived in North Carolina.

One way we taught our children was by having preachers come over for a meal and a time of fellowship in God's Word. In our church, whoever preached always went to Sunday lunch at somebody's house, so we signed up once a month so I could teach my children hospitality and have them interact with these godly men. Those times of fellowship gave us all a chance to ask questions about the part of the Bible we'd been studying and talk about it. It was a neat way to bring the kids up.

The ladies at that church were collecting things for missionaries all over the world. There was a brochure, Workers Together, that went out from Wheaton Bible College every other month. It would list missionaries all over the world. The brochure included things that they needed personally or things they needed for the ministry. The ladies would collect the donations, but nobody knew how to ship them. Shipping internationally is complicated. It's different for every country—what's needed, how to ship it.

At that particular time, I was doing architectural drafting and office design for a company that sets up dental offices in North Carolina and South Carolina. I had started working in my dad's dental office when I was nine years old, so I knew what dentists and dental technicians needed and what the front office required. Plus, there are many special requirements for electrical and wall materials when you have different power equipment and X-ray shielding to consider. I got special certifications for some of that.

We had a shipping department at that company. So, I went to my boss and I said, "Hey, can I use the shipping department on my lunch break? I'll pay for everything. I'll bring on my own supplies." He agreed, and that helped me. I started learning how to ship internationally and fill out all the customs forms. Because of that, the ministry started internationally. We didn't know we were starting a ministry, we were just being obedient. So, I want to tell the young people reading this that God will work in small things, and He can start them even now in your life. If He can trust you with something small, He will continue to give more and more and more and more.

So, God used something I had from my job to help move those shipments to different missionaries and missions organizations. That was one small thing that God had put in my life that made a big difference. My husband and I still just really felt God was calling us to go into missions and we battled it for a long time. But in the meantime, I'm like, "Okay, God, I'm gonna be obedient to what you've given me to do at this moment at this time, and maybe this is the stepping stone to go to a different country and serve you."

Blessings from the Breezeway

So, I already mentioned that the ladies in my church were collecting things for missionaries. I'd get copy paper boxes, cover them with contact paper, and line them up against the wall in the Sunday school room, so it was easy for them to remember. Then, I would bring the things home, package them in my breezeway, and get them sorted. The breezeway was where my laundry was at, and I had a little table with all the craft things—Playdough and things like that—where my kids would play while I did my work. It was just a small room, six by ten feet, but it was enough then.

One of the things we collected was canceled stamps. A family in Canada would sell them to Canadian stamp collectors because, back then, the only way you could get US stamps was for somebody to bring them in. And all the money they raised went to support the printing ministry of a family in Bolivia. They would make between three and five thousand dollars a year selling US stamps.

Another thing we sent was layette sets. One lady would make blankets and go around to yard sales and get onesies, put them in a Ziploc bag, and call them layette sets. We would send them to a particular mission hospital in Chavuma, Zambia, Africa and they would give them to new mothers. Every time a woman would have a baby, they would give them one of those.

Then they would say, "If you bring your child back for all their immunizations, then when their immunizations are complete when the baby turns two years old, we'll give you another outfit."

Women would walk sometimes ten or fifteen miles from their villages to make sure that they got those immunizations. When they would come for the immunizations, then the mission would use that opportunity to teach them about hygiene—taking care of their bodies, preventing pregnancies . . . you know, giving your body a rest. They would teach all these things healthwise, but they would also do Bible studies with them.

After about twenty years of doing this, the government came to this mission-run hospital to find out what they were doing. The government could see there was about a twenty-mile radius around the hospital where children weren't dying from childhood diseases anymore. They wanted to know how they were accomplishing it.

The missionaries explained. Well, we give them an outfit. We give them a completion of their immunizations. They'll come for the whole series since they know there's a reward at the end.

That's how they wiped out childhood diseases in that area now and since then. The government been involved for over fifteen years now and is using the concept the missionaries brought to wipe out childhood diseases in Africa.

The amount of donations kept growing, and eventually, the breezeway wasn't big enough. I went from managing the collections in my breezeway to using a Sunday school room, then two, then three.

Then my accident happened.

The Wreck: Miracles in the Midst of Tragedy

That day, Aug. 22, 2002, I was headed out to pick up a donation from the Bob Barker company and drop some stuff off at church. In case you don't know, the Bob Barker Co. isn't related to Bob Barker from *The Price is Right*. This company is a family-owned corrections supply business based right here in North Carolina. They've been a very generous supporter of our ministry for years.

So, our next-door neighbor had a box truck, and the year before, he'd picked up a bunch of boxes for me and dropped them off at a ministry in New York when he was traveling to visit family. This year,

I was picking up the boxes, and I planned to shrink-wrap them onto a pallet so he could easily unload them in New York. He was going sixty miles out of his way to drop these off for us, so I wanted to make it as easy as possible for him.

The plan was to send the kids over to their grandparents. Our 10-year-old daughter Amy was going to spend the day with her grandmother learning to sew, and Ashley Jr., thirteen, would go shooting on the range with her grandfather while I drove the truck over to the Bob Barker plant in Fuquay-Varina, got it loaded, then brought it all back.

We got off to a late start. We were just getting ready to sit down and eat before we left when Amy came running through the house. Then she hit her toe on the baseboard, fell down, and started crying.

We finished lunch and rode up to the neighbor's house on our four-wheeler to pick up the truck. Heading off to their grandparents, we got out on Highway 421, past Campbell University, and I came up behind an eighteen-wheeler in the right lane. He moved into the left lane, which is where you expect truckers to be at that point because most truckers turn left onto another highway. I'm in the right lane, and suddenly he makes a right turn in front of me.

I turned right, too, hoping to avoid t-boning him, but my truck hit the right rear corner of his cab, and he just kept going. He claimed he didn't feel anything. The movement pulled the front end of the box truck up on the frame rail that runs between the cab and the dump trailer he was hauling. Both my front wheels were off the ground, the back wheels were on the road, and he just kept going.

Once he finally stopped and got out, I couldn't put the truck in park. The key was broken and the ignition was jammed. The first wrecker on the scene was trying to get under our truck to clip the lines.

The trucker looked in at us through the busted windshield and asked, "Y'all OK?" I did not know at the time that you could not even recognize me as a person, because I was covered in blood and glass from head to toe. My daughter was bleeding from cuts in her eye. Ashley was the only one who looked alright.

"Are y'all ok? Do you need anything?" the truck driver said. But by then, the police and the EMS had arrived. It turns out that this guy had just gotten his CDL [Commercial Drivers License] back after spending eighteen months in jail for DUIs.

"She should have known to stay out of my way," he told the police. The huge God moment was that he'd just confirmed his insurance policy with the trucking company that day. So he couldn't claim he was uninsured.

My husband was driving a 52-foot flatbed just three miles down the road when our son called him to say what happened. He turned the truck around in a field, drove it straight back to the plant, and took another guy's pickup truck to where I was still pinned. I was pinned in that smashed box truck for an hour and twenty-eight minutes. They had twenty-eight rescue people, all at a loss for how to get me out of there. My left foot was mangled and all tangled up in the metal, my foot twisted entirely backwards. My right leg was pinned between the steering column and the dog box, which houses the motor.

The steering wheel was cradled up against me like it was holding my pregnant belly, so it was like my baby Luke was resting on the steering wheel itself. I need you to know: that was a miracle itself since the steering wheel in that truck sits much higher. God placed that steering wheel lower in that moment so it protected me and my unborn child—not by breaking it off the steering column, just by miraculously moving it when we needed it moved.

The rescue people thought maybe they'd get a crane, cut the top off the cab, and lift me up. I knew that was not a good idea, and I told them so.

"You are not doing that to me," I said. "My leg is not going up. If you get this door open a bit more you can get me onto a backboard."

As quickly as Dad heard the news, he and Mom got to the scene. Dad, being a doctor, had no trouble talking his way inside the line and getting up to the truck where he could see me and talk with me.

"You've always been my little fighter and my little bulldog," he told me. "You're going to be fine." He didn't tell me you couldn't recognize me as a person at that point.

It only takes an hour to cook a chicken; my leg was pinned for an hour and a half against the motor housing. That thing gets hot as fire, and I was burned black pretty near to the bone by the time they got me out. I had to close my eyes and concentrate on my breathing. The hot housing would singe the nerve in my leg, and it felt like a rush of blood.

Now, besides my Dad looking at me through the shattered windshield and talking, there was another gentleman talking to me the whole time. The EMS thought I was crazy; maybe I hurt even worse than they could see because I was talking and no one was standing next to me. As a Life Flight helicopter took off from nearby, the gentleman told me, "That's your daughter. She's going to Duke, and she's going to get to Duke before you do." Nobody at the scene had that information, and I didn't even know yet what kinds of injuries Amy had. And he told me that there was a place over my stomach where we'd be able to see the covering of an angel's wings. Everything else was blood. But the gentleman said God had protected that young man who was going to be born and that God was going to use him in a mighty way.

As Amy's flight went out, I told the EMS team, "I don't want to go to Duke."

"Ma'am, when there's trauma at this location, you're Life-Flighted to Duke," one of the attendants told me.

"When are you going to be done so I can go home?" I asked.

"Ma'am, you're not going home today," he said.

It's a good thing that God gives you just what you need at that moment. If I had known what I had in front of me, I might have given up.

I'd turned thirty-eight just a month before. And I was twenty-three weeks pregnant with our third child. They finally got me out and Life Flighted me to Duke Trauma Center.

* * *

Medically, I began baffling the doctors right from the start. I heard people around my hospital bed saying things like, "Man, we still don't know why you're still here, why you're still breathing." Someone told me directly, "We don't know why you didn't die in that hour and a half it took them to cut you out of that vehicle. We can't explain why you're still alive."

Among my long list of injuries was a lacerated spleen. Besides the two shattered legs and the severe burn, my spleen had been sliced in two by the impact. You usually die within the first hour after this kind of injury if it hasn't been treated, but somehow, I had made it through ninety minutes trapped in the vehicle and the trip to the hospital. A nurse came in and ultrasounded my spleen at eleven o'clock at night. What she saw didn't make sense to her.

"All your vitals are normal," she said. She couldn't believe it. She started coming in to check me hourly. At seven the next morning, I had another ultrasound. When the nurse saw the results, she called the doctors in. "There's nothing wrong with her spleen," she told them. "If I didn't take both of those ultrasounds myself, I wouldn't believe this. It is completely healed."

The doctors looked at the ultrasounds and said, "We cannot explain this. Your spleen is lacerated; usually, in this condition, you would die within an hour, and that hasn't happened."

"God didn't bring me through this and protect this baby just for me to lose it now," I said.

Well, God still does miracles. Here's one more amazing thing. When the orphanage in South India that this load was intended for heard what had happened, they gathered everyone in the chapel center, and they all prayed. That's about 350 people. They are in a different time zone, so they were praying from 11 p.m. to 7 a.m. Exactly the same eight hours between the ultrasound that showed my spleen lacerated and the ultrasound that showed it completely healed. Like I said, God still does miracles!

That said, I still had a fractured right femur. I had a crushed foot that was totally turned in the other direction—the bones were shattered into little pieces like Rice Krispies. And there was that huge burn that later healed in the shape of a heart.

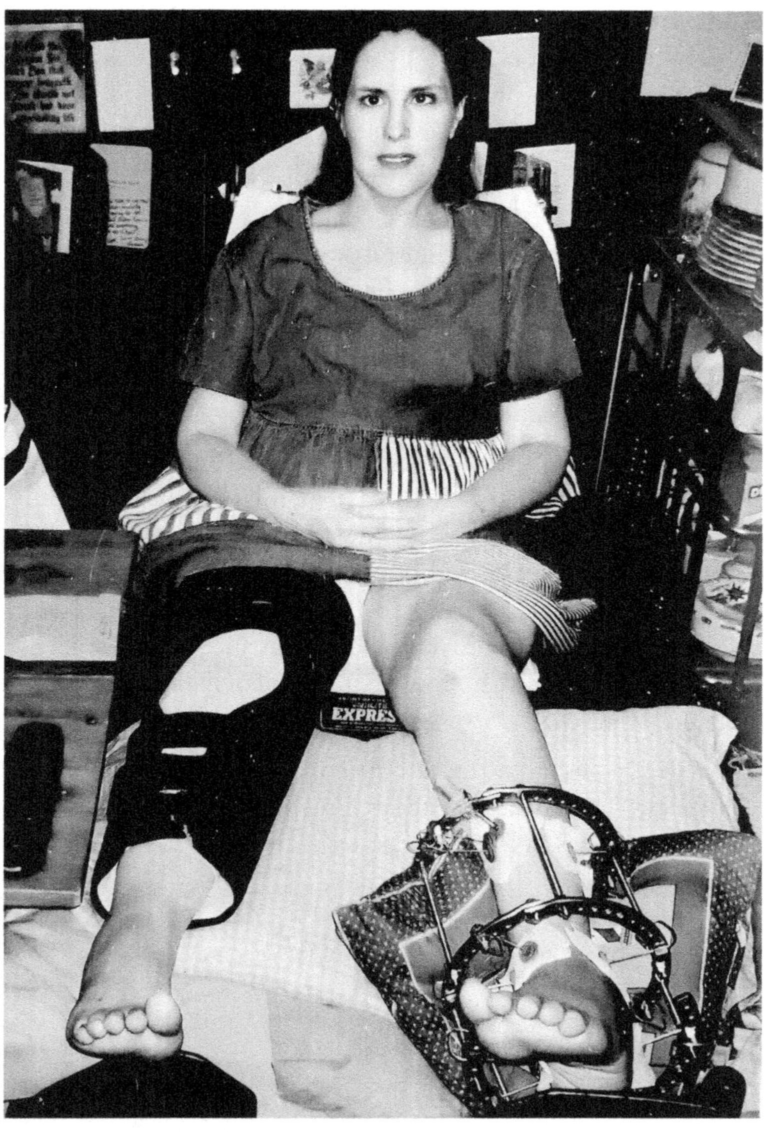

I needed two different surgeries to start with, and because my injuries were so severe, the doctor wouldn't let me be moved to a hospital
closer to home. I needed to stay in the trauma unit, they said. They

limited anesthesia to protect the baby, but he didn't miss a beat. He was just moving all over the place.

My angel came into the room to see me and told me a few things about how my daughter was doing. During her ambulance ride, she had been praying with her stuffed piglet that she'd carried with her that day. During the first ambulance ride to the local hospital, before the flight to Duke, she'd been healed of the medical condition she had before the accident. She didn't have any fluid in her pelvic cavity anymore.

The nurse told me there was no one in the room, and there's not been one visitor that morning.

I spent fourteen days in the hospital, and then after that they sent an ambulance weekly to my home to bring me in for treatments. I couldn't ride in a car yet. That year, I had three surgeries between August and October, and I had surgery every year for fifteen years after. That means I'm in a wheelchair three months a year. And we still continued to run the ministry.

Satan's a slow learner. He tried to take me out with an eighteen-wheeler and he just didn't understand: I'm not going to quit.

> **Satan's a slow learner. He tried to take me out with an 18-wheeler and he just didn't understand: I'm not going to quit.**

Miracles in the Ministry:

This ministry started in the breezeway of our home, where we had kept a few boxes for the things the ladies at church collected for missionaries. Then, we got space in the back of our church, and we were there for twenty-one years. Then in August 2018, we got the warehouse we're in now. It's 17,000 square feet, and at first, you could drive your car in it to park. We drove trucks into it. Kids played on scooters and skateboards in there. And now it's so full that you have to turn sideways to get in there because God has filled it up.

So that is how the ministry started. And God just grew it and grew it. We're getting ready to ship our thirty-sixth container in a year to Ukraine, and we've shipped to 104 countries around the world.

Making What's Needed

A lot of times, we don't know how God is going to use something someone has donated. And a lot of times, God can surprise us with how they'll be used.

One donation we receive consistently is damaged and discarded prison uniforms. We get all the UPS damaged and other discards coming out of the Bob Barker Co., which supplies correctional facilities all over the US. Well, from the smalls to the 2XLs, we ship as clothing. The elastic waist pants and the V-neck tops look like medical scrubs. We send them into Zambia and that's what they're used as. They don't care that they have stripes or even sometimes prison names on them. They're just glad to have some clothes.

But for the larger ones, sized 3XL up to 16XL, we cut them into yards and yards of amazing fabric that sews great. My mother came up with the idea in 2012 to make that fabric into Bible bags. In many other countries, they always carry their Bible and hymn book together, and it's very important to them that they have something to carry them in.

At first, we made them for Operation Mobilization ships. Now we ship them everywhere, and they're used in all different ways. Campbell University Medical School takes them on their medical mission trips. When a mom comes into the clinic with three or four kids, they're all going to need something different. So, to make sure mom gets the right medicine for the right child, they color code the kid's hands and medicine jars. They put it in one of these bags, hand each child a salvation doll, and are off.

We make hygiene kits for people who are homeless, in nursing homes, for those who've been in house fires, for places where there have been disasters and wars. So we put hygiene kits in these bags. We put school supplies in them. To date, more than 46,000 of these have been made by my mother and others, and she's kept up with where every one of them has gone. You can sew them at home yourself on your own time and serve the Lord. And we don't waste a scrap!

We send whatever is left after the bags are made to other ministries in our community. So, we have one church that makes fidget quilts for Alzheimer's units. We have another one that makes adult bibs for people in nursing homes or special needs adults served by missions. We also have quilting groups that use the big-enough scraps to make quilts. All different things can be done with the fabric. We also ship the fabric with sewing machines to orphanages so they can make what they need.

The Gospel Always Goes Forth

The Gospel goes out with everything we send out. We give people the Gospel of John. It's not too much to read, so they're going to read it. They're going to read John 3:16.

If we don't have a tract or a Gospel in the right language for the country, we put in a card from Transworld Radio that has a QR code. When you pull it up on your phone, somehow it knows what language you speak, so you don't have to search a website. It's gonna come up in your language, so everyone can do Bible studies. They can request prayer. It's just pretty amazing.

We see a lot of Gospel outreach locally through Campbell University. Their medical school does more outreach in our community than any church I've found so far.

They go out into the migrant camps every Monday night and provide medical care. They go to different camps in Harnett, Johnson, and Lee counties—they cover them all. They also do a clinic on Tuesday nights for the uninsured of Harnett County and on Wednesday nights in Cumberland County. They do a lot of outreach. They use medical care as their platform to share the Gospel of Jesus Christ. We provide hygiene kits and suitcases to them. The conditions of the people that live in the camps are unbelievable. Sometimes that suitcase becomes a dresser drawer. So, what comes to us is used in a lot of different ways.

The Warehouse Brings Christians Together

We started praying for a warehouse, not just because there were so many donations, but also because we needed more volunteers. Nobody would volunteer at my church because it wasn't their church or their denomination. And we kept praying, "Lord, we need a warehouse. We need something without a steeple. We need something without a church name on the door because all of our church names are just names that we're worshiping under now. There's not going to be Baptist, Methodist, Catholic, whatever, in heaven. We're all believers and part of the same family of Jesus Christ if we know Jesus as our Savior."

Almost as soon as we got into the warehouse, Hurricane Florence hit. People had been going stir-crazy just waiting for the hurricane to land, and once it did, it went viral that we needed help to get loads of emergency supplies out to the airport. So I rolled up the doors of my warehouse that day and there were a hundred people standing out front, ready to help. I had everybody sign in with their name and what church they were from, and I only knew ten of these people. There were people from six different denominations, some of them people who were staying with relatives because they were evacuated.

People from all backgrounds have come in to volunteer. I've had church groups and high school student groups, people from all kinds of denominations and religious backgrounds. In fact, God set it up to complete the move from the church into the warehouse with help from an Australian family I met online that was traveling across the country to see the US. We've had volunteers come to Christ, and we've had young people ask to know more about Jesus, because I give the plan of salvation in my presentation to every new group of volunteers.

God Gives Us a Name

We still didn't have a name for what we were doing. I kept trying to name it, and we just kept calling it "the mission room."

Well, finally, God gave us the name of Crossing All Borders International. And we felt like it represented what God had been allowing us to be a part of. Crossing All Borders represents that we cross geographic, ethnic, economic, educational, and denominational borders. You have to understand that this is not my ministry. This is God's ministry. He gives me the privilege to oversee it.

We Know It's God Because What We're Doing is Impossible!

We know that this is God's work because what we do is not humanly possible.

Here in the US, we're used to thinking we can just go to the post office, FedEx, or the UPS Store and ship things anywhere. But international shipping isn't that easy. Part of how God trained me for this ministry was getting me started shipping ministry stuff from the shipping department of a company where I used to work. I learned a lot about international shipping there. Every country has different rules and limits, and you have to learn those to get something there from here.

But lots of countries are even harder to ship into. One of the impossible things God has allowed us to do is ship into countries with very limited access whether because of war, disasters, or corruption and bribery. Here are just a couple of those miracle stories.

The Impossible is Possible: Haiti

There's no way to ship anything into Haiti. You can't send a container in there. If you ship a box there, the people it's addressed to will never see it. But God connected us with someone who knew how.

This man was at a missions conference in Myrtle Beach and was talking with people about some of the items his ministry, Sea Hope, wanted to take on a mission in Haiti. And the guy next to him slipped my card to him and said, "Call this lady. I bet she can find what you need."

Buddy and Mary Puryear from Sea Hope came and met with me. The Sea Hope was built as a US Navy training ship. It has twenty-four bunks and can carry a whole container, and the Puryears were shipping containers by way of Puerto Rico because they couldn't get them directly into Haiti. In Haiti, there's no government whatsoever. Whatever you send there, it just sails right into junk mail or someone's back pocket. The only way we found to get something into Haiti is to send it to the Sea Hope ship.

So, with Sea Hope, we've been able to equip a hospital in Haiti. The doctor who had built the hospital ran it for thirty years, but it fell into disarray after he left. I was privileged to get to go recently and sail on that ship to deliver a container to Haiti.

One of the things that we took on that ship was an ultrasound machine we had. We'd tried to donate it to a local ministry and then to a ministry in Honduras. Every time we tried to get it into Honduras, God closed the door, and that thing was in the warehouse for three years. We kept moving it around when it got in the way. We kept saying, "Lord, when is this going to go?"

And then we were packing our second container for Haiti. Buddy mentioned that they would love to get some other larger medical items for the NICU (Neonatal Intensive Care Unit) they were trying to set up. One of the items he listed was an ultrasound machine. "We'd love to get an ultrasound machine. They've never seen a baby before it's born in Haiti."

"I've got an ultrasound machine," I told him.

"You're kidding!" he said.

I told him, "We've been trying to figure out where God wants us to send that."

So, we packed it for the container going to Haiti.

We made it to Haiti. And a while after I got back, I received a video of the ultrasound machine being used, and for the first time doctors and mothers saw a child before it's born. They've seen a heartbeat and life in a way they've never seen before. I get chills thinking about it. That's only God. He saved that ultrasound machine for such a time as this. He knew exactly when I received it exactly where it was going in the end.

So, that's another thing that I had to learn: sometimes God gives us stuff. And we have to wait on His time because He knows exactly where it's supposed to be going. We just have to trust Him 100 percent.

The Impossible is Possible: Ukraine

When we started shipping to Ukraine during the war, we thought it would be a really big deal to do three containers. At that time, these containers cost $6,000 a piece to ship (now it's $8,000) and that's a lot of money. It's not the kind of money we were used to seeing in our ministry. But God connected me with pastor Andriy Ivanets, from Ukraine, who pastors Living Waters Church in Greensboro, North Carolina. We've been working together on this whole thing. Twenty-six members of his church decided to hold a prayer meeting, and to their surprise, 250 people showed up. Within fourteen days, they had $125,000 in their account and we had $38,000 at Crossing All Borders.

I don't even know where all the churches are that the money came from. We combined our funds, purchased medications and military gear, and shipped sixteen containers.

About that time, the pastor of a Ukrainian church in Ohio reached out to Andriy. He asked if Andriy's church could send money to help his congregation with the cost of shipping essentials to Ukraine. They had already shipped more than thirty containers and were looking for other Ukrainian churches to help with the costs.

When Andriy explained what we had been doing, Pastor Victor was amazed. "You are getting all the types of items that are needed," he said. "You keep shipping and just bill it to us! "

We continued shipping and sharing resources for months. One day, on the way to ship container number thirty-one, Andriy told his team that funds were running low, so he was unsure how many more shipments could be made. Shortly after they arrived at our warehouse, he received a text from Pastor Victor.

A businessman had asked Victor, "How are you doing for money?" and when Victor described the need, he responded immediately, "I'm getting you a $60,000 cashier's check so you can continue shipping. Tell me when that's gone so I can send you more."

Andriy was excited to tell me this "God story" and also shook his head at himself. "I have so little faith!" he said.

That Ukrainian congregation in Ohio and their contacts have paid for containers seventeen through thirty-six—so far!

Now mind you, we did this ministry for thirty-four years with no money, and we still do this ministry with no income. So, we started bringing in some money and we still always say, "You know God's gonna provide what we need."

But shipping costs aren't the only thing that makes it hard to send things into Ukraine. Our first container got canceled four times, and Andriy found out why. The shipping rules had suddenly changed, and the only people who could receive a container in Ukraine were people in political office. But Andriy has a friend who is the mayor of a city in Ukraine. Everyone made fun of him when he ran for office; Andriy says "I now see God prepared him to be a modern-day Joseph."

In Ukraine, a mayor is responsible for the churches in the community as well as the government resources we think about. So this particular mayor had stockpiled Bibles against a future need before the war even started! God put him in that position for such a time as this, and every one of our containers goes to him. They go into Poland, then are trucked into Ukraine.

And the churches are having a mass impact. They're out in the streets just playing their guitars, meeting in groups, and singing to Jesus. And then they're handing out Bibles. I didn't know there was a Russian Bible Society, but they contacted me. They had over 3,000 Bibles in Ukraine and over 250,000 tracts in Ukrainian and those go in every box and every hygiene kit they put together in Ukraine. So the people who put them together get to handle those Bibles and tracts.

We thought we'd be doing just a few containers, but God opened the door, and we sent thirty-six containers in just a year. It has become like a container weekly we can ship out. It's just been a God thing, and He continues to provide the funds. It's amazing what God is doing in Ukraine and we're just sitting there and all going there's no other way this could happen. There's none of us here that could do this. Only God could do this. So, we are tremendously blessed to do so much. It is such a privilege to be used by God in this way.

When the Bob Barker Co. first gave us this building to use, there was no rent, no water bill, and no light bill. Bob sold the building but made arrangements for us to continue to stay in the building. Now, we pay rent to a management company, and Bob offered to pay it for us. But I say, "Why would I go to Bob to pay my rent when I can go to the God that made the whole universe?" What God has given us is everything we need—the whole warehouse, every shelf, cart, forklift, pallet jack—it's unbelievable.

We Know It's God Because Even the Oddest Donation is Actually Needed

Sometimes, we pray for something, and we have to wait for God to send it. Other times, God gives us something and we have to wait to use it. But if God gave it, we wait until God shows us how He plans to use it. I already told you about those thirteen pallets of neckties. We'd been able to send some of them over to places like Zambia, where the men love to get them to dress up for church. Some local churches used them in their Easter cantatas or other productions. But most of them were just sitting on the pallets, waiting for God to show us what to do.

And then came the war in Ukraine, and you know the rest of the story. A doctor in Nebraska told us that neckties worked great as tourniquets, and those neckties became tourniquets at a time when there were no tourniquets to be had anywhere in the world. God knew when they'd be needed and how they'd be used. We just had to wait on His timing.

A good many years ago, we had a group of young men in our church who were going on a mission trip. This was back before there were cell phones or computers for communicating with the missionaries. You had to wait on a letter in the mail any time you wanted to connect with them.

So, a year before they were due to head out, I told them, "You need to get me a list of what is needed so I can give you anything I have. That way, you can use your money on what we don't have." They were going to be doing construction and we didn't have hammers and nails, so they knew they'd have to buy those. If they needed clothes and shoes, we could have helped, but three weeks before they left, we still didn't have a list. They said they were waiting on a letter from the missionary.

At the same time, we had somebody who would drop things off at the church's backdoor for us. We had no idea who was doing this. It was often brand new stuff, tags still on it—sometimes there was even cash in there. It was months before I caught this person and found out who they were.

But one Tuesday, I showed up and there were two big black trash bags, heavy and full, at the back door. I opened them and there was nothing inside but deep sea fishing line. This is some high-dollar stuff, I gotta tell you. And I'm thinking, "What am I going to do with this stuff?"

Well this is a really good example of a time when God gave us stuff and we didn't have any idea why He's given it. We were laughing and wondering, "What are we going to do with this?" We had a barrel that we called God's Barrel. It was for items that were donated that we had no idea how anyone could use them. Whenever we get something that we have no idea how God wants us to use it, we put it in God's Barrel and wait.

So, the boys got back to us just a few days before they were due to head off to Suriname. They approached me and said, "Hey Miss Joeth, I finally know what we need. It's something you probably don't have."

And I just said: "Try God: It might already be in His barrel."

And what did they need? Fishing line. Because in Surinam, fishing is how they stay alive. That's how they don't starve to death.

So they took two fifty-pound bags of fishing line with them.

Twenty-four years later, we ran into a friend, Ted McKenny, at church. We've known Ted for years from different things in the community. And it turns out he was the missionary the boys were helping in Suriname.

God knows what is needed and where it's needed. We just send it along.

> **God knows what is needed and where it's needed. We just send it along.**

Maturing in Faith Through God's Miracles

My childhood church was very legalistic, and that impacted my faith—I could never keep all those rules! I remember the day some of the families got together to pick the excess butter beans at someone's farm. Mom grew up on a hog farm in Iowa, so she knew what it's like to work on a farm. She put me in shorts and a tank top, so I'd be comfortable to work. And one of the deacons' wives pulled my mother aside and told her what the rules about girls' clothing were. We went home, and she took all my shorts, anything sleeveless, out of my bureau. I was only six years old, and I remember it like it was yesterday.

In my teen years, I had a youth pastor whose wife wore slacks. She let us know that sometimes a dress isn't more modest. If you're playing softball, it's hard to run from base to base and be modest when your skirts are flying up. If you've gone on a trip to the amusement park, you can't wear a dress and be modest while you ride a roller coaster!

So, at first I was taught to only wear dresses, and then I was taught that modesty was what mattered. Like I said, it was hard to keep track of all the rules. Over time, I've learned that God doesn't care about some things as much as some churches do. What matters is that we care about God and do what God wants us to do.

Shouldn't I Be a Missionary?

Since I was saved on the mission field, I kept thinking I was supposed to be a missionary. And we kept getting large donations of things that could make a big impact on one particular mission organization: Operation Mobilization. The goal of OM is to make sure there's a community of Christians within reach of every person around the world. OM has four ships that carry their workers and supplies around the globe. They've got more than 4,900 missionaries who come from 118 countries serving in 120 countries. A lot of what we were getting from Bob Barker was stuff their ships could use. We were sending OM at least two 20-foot container loads a year of stuff that they'd have to purchase if we didn't give it to them. A little later, when they got the newest ship, Logos Hope, we were instrumental in providing towels, soaps, and sheets to fit it out.

So, all of those shipments got our attention focused on OM. And we just really felt God was calling us to this ministry. Eventually, my husband and I went down to Florence, South Carolina to talk with them about being missionaries.

I'll never forget it. We were sitting across the table from Miles Te-ows, who's their vice president for partner development. We told him, "You know, we feel like God's calling us to come here." And he looked at me and looked at my husband, and he said, "Well, what's going to happen to everybody else if you leave your ministry and join ours? You know, you save our ministry over half a million dollars a year by giving us things that without you, we'd have to buy out of money we raise."

Then he went wide. He said, "What's going to happen to all the ministries that you're having an impact on if all of a sudden you go to one location?"

And that's when God opened our eyes and showed us that no matter where we were, we are all missionaries. When you become a believer in Jesus Christ, you are a missionary. There are people that you will reach that I can't reach, there's people I will reach that you can't reach. We're all uniquely made and God has made us—if you want to say it that way—peculiar people. He has somebody specific that you can minister to that nobody else can. Everyone who accepts Jesus Christ, even if you never leave where you grew up, you're still serving God on foreign soil because this is not your home. So, we are all missionaries. And that's when we just settled that God was using us to reach many nations instead of one nation.

What God told us is, "Instead of sending you one place to serve, I'm sending you to many nations. Whether you're shipping a box or a container, whether for a church mission trip, a local ministry, or Operation Mobilization, I want you to impact many. Not just one area."

I'd thought this was just a stepping stone that God was using to teach me something I'd take elsewhere. But no. God said He was building it for something I couldn't even imagine.

A Growing Faith

For me growing up, I was always worried about whether I was saved. Am I saved, or am I not saved? If I thought I had really screwed up, I figured there's no chance. People were always making a big deal about what they could see was wrong in your life, but it's not their job to convict you. God's the one who's got to convict you. There might be something else that God thinks is more important that God wants to change first. And no one ever gets everything right.

The Bible says Christ had to die on the cross because the law could not be kept, no matter how hard you try. In the Bible, Jesus says, "I give them eternal life, and they shall never perish; no one will snatch them out of my hand" John 10:28 (NIV). Even you can't pluck yourself out of God's hands!

God created us, gave us life, died on the cross, gave us eternal life, and then He uses us. We get to be His hands and His feet and His mouth, if we just say, "Here I am Lord, use me." But He's a gentleman: He's drawing you to Him, He's not going to force Himself on you. And He's not going to force you to do the works.

But He will give you the power to do the works. It might be power from gifts and talents God has given you. It might be power from skills God has let you learn. It might be power by way of helpers and donors God sends to you. And that's what we've seen. I have disabilities from that accident. It takes me some time to get started in the morning. I take medications, and it took nineteen surgeries spread over fifteen years to be able to walk. Still, God has given the power to do this ministry.

After the wreck, I was told I was doing way too well. I would eventually hit a wall, people said. And they were right. I spent two and a half years in the deepest, darkest depression. But it wasn't because of the accident. It was because of another big loss in our life.

Walking in Grace, Not Grief

When people read about all the miracles in my life, sometimes they think I don't have challenges. Or maybe they think I'm just a special person who has so much faith I don't ever get bothered by challenges. Those aren't really true.

I have tons of the craziest stories possible, because I have the kind of life where if something can go wrong it will. It might be a little thing, like a spider egg sack on the ceiling busting open and dropping thousands of baby spiders onto our pizza when we're on a date. It might be a big thing, like getting both of my legs smashed in an accident when I'm going to pick up a donation.

If anyone tells you your life is going to be easy from now on, Satan's going to say, "Let me see how I can cause discord and trouble." What I have had to learn is to walk in God's grace, even while the challenges are still flying all around me.

When Ashley and I lost our business and our home back when the economy crashed in 2008, that was a big challenge that I didn't do so well with. When Ashley died in 2021, that was a big challenge, and

God had put things in place to help me cope. We lived every bit of our marriage vows—for richer and for poorer, in sickness and health. Let me tell you a little more about our love story, our life challenges, and how God helped.

A Love Story

I met my husband Ashley when I was fifteen years old at New Life Bible Camp in Raleigh, North Carolina. I started going there every summer starting when I was in third grade, in 1973. If you could memorize 300 Bible verses, you could earn a week at camp, and I was determined, so that's how I went.

The year when I was fifteen, I spotted Ashley at camp and I heard God say, "That's going to be your husband one day." But Ashley didn't hear the same thing at all! He thought I was very stuck up. At the end of camp, everybody was passing their addresses around so they could be pen pals. I noticed one of my friends wasn't paying attention as he put his address on her pile, so I managed to sneak it out.

He didn't even remember who I was. I wrote him, and he clearly didn't know who it was. He wrote back and asked for my picture. We decided we were just writing as friends, and then he suggested we become prayer partners. So we did that for a year.

What I hadn't figured out was that Ashley's aunt and uncle lived near us and went to the same church my family did. So on May 12, 1980, I got a phone call from him in the afternoon. "I'm at my aunt and uncle's," he said. "Are you coming to church tonight?"

Now, my parents had a strict rule that I could not date until I was sixteen. I was still only fifteen—I would turn sixteen in July—so I just figured I'd go sit by myself at church, and maybe he'd come sit with me.

My parents met him that night and they decided to break their rule. "You can't date until you're sixteen," they said, "but we'll let you date him."

He lived more than an hour away in Youngsville, so we didn't see each other every day, and we couldn't talk often either. Back then, calling that far was an actual long-distance call that cost money. His dad would allow him to call once a week on Saturday to decide what we were going to do together on Sunday. We worked out a plan that gave us the most time we could get. He'd meet me at our church in Raleigh, come over to the house and eat lunch, then we'd do something on Sunday afternoon.

After church on Sunday night, the youth would always go out for pizza. That's how we dated for two years. Our first real date was at the Wake Christian Academy athletic banquet, which I was invited to because I kept the books for one of the teams.

He gave me a diamond in September of my senior year. That did not go well with my parents, because by then they'd realized his parents were divorced. We were not allowed to have friends whose parents were divorced, and my parents felt like I had deceived them. Of course, I didn't know his parents were divorced at first either. I'd never been exposed to divorce, so when he talked about spending the weekend at his mom's, it didn't click with me.

It also turns out that my mother had her heart set on me and my sister marrying pastors, and Ashley wasn't going to be a pastor. But Ashley turned out to have a real pastor's heart, and after he died, it surprised my father how many lives he had affected just as a regular church member.

Three of those years we dated, we were both in high school. Then, we both went to tech school and had one year of programs. I took mechanical drafting and engineering on a scholarship for women going into nontraditional careers. He was doing a pilot program for diesel engine repair. We saw each other on campus, then got married on May 19, 1984.

Except for two rough years, our marriage was really good. I attribute that to being friends and prayer partners first. Being in a long-distance relationship was an added benefit because we each had our own lives. He had his own church, extracurricular activities, and sports. I had the same. That was always a strength in our marriage, not like some other couples where one person always wants to know what the other is doing. No matter how old you are or how young you are, you always have to have people other than your spouse in your life. We ran a business together, but we both had friends outside the marriage. You go through times when you need people outside the marriage. I wouldn't be making it now after my husband's death if I didn't have friends outside my marriage.

The Miracle of Our Children

Starting when I was a teenager, I was getting these cysts on each ovary, and they would rupture and form scar tissue each time. I was told back then that I probably would not be able to have children, and when we got married, the doctor said the chances of you having children is pretty slim.

When we first got married, I went for two years without a period and another three years with infertility. We started adoption proceedings, and then like it sometimes happens, I got pregnant. And I miscarried. Then two weeks after the miscarriage I got pregnant with our oldest son, Ashley III. A little over two years later, we got pregnant with Amy. And then we got pregnant again, and we miscarried that child. So, we decided we just needed to be content with what God had given us. And we went back to preventing pregnancy.

But God saw otherwise. And when God wants you to get pregnant, you're going to get pregnant. That's when I got pregnant with Luke. That's why there's such an age difference between our children. They were thirteen and ten when I got pregnant with Luke, and Luke was the one I was pregnant with when I had the accident. You already know that he was miraculously protected in that collision, and now he's an adult.

The Perfect Storm

There were two years when our marriage was a challenge. Some of it was our own doing, but some of it was just that perfect storm.

Ashley had been working as a diesel mechanic and got a chance to own his own truck. He bought the Peterbilt cab on a handshake from someone he'd done work for, then he got a dump trailer and he hauled sand and rock and things like that for a company that manufactures concrete products. Then, he got a flatbed and was hauling brick and block for a company that built houses.

I stayed at home because he didn't want me to work, but we continued to struggle with the business and our finances. Ashley had always wanted me to handle the money—he didn't want to see it or hear about it. So, I was drowning in worry. We got heavily into debt trying to run the company. We were buried under credit cards because we used them to pay for the truck fuel and other business stuff. I got so depressed I didn't even make our credit card payments. We couldn't pay our mortgage either.

We should have quit the business sooner. My husband was a good worker, but he wasn't a go-getter when it came to finding work and business. We were ninety-some thousand in debt when he finally sold the truck and went back to work as a mechanic.

In the meantime, we'd gotten into some bad investments by following a financial advisor who actually destroyed us. We didn't believe in bankruptcy and kept trying to pay things off, but eventually, we realized we could continue down this path until we're ninety and still not come even. So, we got ourselves declared bankrupt. We hired an auction company to come in and auction off 80 percent of what we owned and moved from our house on thirteen acres to a little 900-square-foot rental, a two-story tobacco barn made into a tiny house, with the upstairs for a guest room and two bedrooms and baths added on opposite ends.

We were there for four years, and we were thankful, the happiest we've ever been. We could see what God had taken us through and we were waiting to see what God was going to do. Then, we moved into another rental that had three bedrooms and two baths. We moved into that house because we were taking care of a little girl while her mama worked full-time and went to nursing school, and it was easier for everyone if they just lived with us.

We told Stephanie that her baby, Lily, was seeing us more than she was seeing of her mama. "We need to get you under the same roof with us, so when you come home from work late she's right there in the same home with you." We charged her minimal rent so she could pay for her schooling as she went. When Stephanie remarried, she moved out, but Ashley still said, "I'm adopting Lily as my granddaughter because my children are taking too long to have grandchildren."

Miracles End a Shorter Storm

Of course, it would be someone else's life if nothing crazy happened next. We'd been looking for three years for a place to buy. We heard that the owner of our rental was thinking about selling, and they gave us the first option, but housing prices were insane. We couldn't do it.

So one day, we get a text from the owner: "Oh, by the way, we need you out of the house in eight weeks."

Eight stinkin' weeks.

A friend of ours had a place she was selling; we shook and sent a contract. Then, four weeks later, she tells us she's not going to sell it.

That left us with twenty-eight days to find something, get a loan, and get our butts out of the rental house.

Our realtor called to say there's a house that meets all your requirements: handicap friendly, four bedrooms and three full baths, in the country; no homeowners association and an acre of land. We jumped on it and scheduled the first appointment in the morning.

Ashley was not impressed with it. It needed too much work. The sheetrock wasn't finished; the painting wasn't done. The realtor suggested we offer less and ask them to finish their projects.

I made an executive decision. If they finished the job, we'd just end up redoing it to our own taste. If we offered less, we might not get the house. A little over 24 hours after the original call, we were under contract.

There were a few other miracles that happened. Ashley had just gotten his old job back at Summit Design and Engineering, so we qualified for the loan. And something happened with the bank rates that helped. Also, I found out about an inheritance I never knew was coming. But here's the big one. We were so ticked when we got kicked out of that rental house! But God knew. If we hadn't been kicked out at that time, we wouldn't have this house. And it's so different from what we owned before or from what we were renting. It's really unbelievable. The house we're in now is handicap friendly. It has a bathroom off the master bedroom. The old house was in a floodplain, and the flooding was terrible.

We did a lot of work with a lot of help to fix this place up, and if it wasn't for that inheritance, we could never have done it. But that was God, sending right what we needed at just the right time. We ripped out all the kitchen cabinets. We took it down to the studs, put in all new electrical, and ripped out the heating ducts to the upstairs. We were moving fast because we wanted to get it done for when Ashley came home from the hospital.

A Fatal Illness

I haven't talked yet about when Ashley got sick. Ashley had diabetes, but he'd been managing it pretty well. On a Tuesday in August, we were scheduled to take him to the doctor thinking his sugars were off because he hadn't been feeling well for a lot of the last week.

Little did we know he actually had COVID. They tested him, and he was positive. A week later, he had to go into the hospital. A little more than a week after that, he had to be moved into the ICU. And he didn't get to come home after that.

Ashley is not the only person we know who died from COVID. There were often cases in our church, five died. Four of his relatives had lung diseases, and only one of them is still alive. So, we know something genetic is why COVID hit him so hard and took his life. He got the treatments, and he told me to put him on the ventilator so I would have no doubt that I had done everything I could medically. But one night, the Lord came to him and told him, "I'm going to take you home."

That sent Ashley into a panic because he was afraid he would die before the children and I could get there. But we had another couple of weeks together, and he was able to tell me how he wanted his things shared among me and the children.

Only Christ holds the key to life and death. God can stop every single death, and not one death happens that God did not allow. God can't cause anything harmful because He's holy and perfect. Anything bad that happens in this world comes from Satan, who lives in this world, and he's loose in this world. So, when people say God didn't answer my prayers, I know that we asked for complete healing, and whether God gave complete healing to stay with his family on Earth or permanently to stay with Him in heaven that's up to God. We did know that if he survived, it would have been a very hard road.

Ashley only got to live in this house from May to August. But one of the things he told me in those last weeks was how he wanted his life insurance payout used. "You promise me," he said, "that you will pay off that house with all of my life insurance, so I know I've provided a home for you that you can't lose." So, through his life insurance after passing, the house is paid for. I'm blessed to have just minimal bills to pay for on a monthly basis.

God put so many things in place that I didn't have an inkling of until my husband died. And then there are the things I know God has put in place, but I haven't seen them yet. So, for example, Ashley was supposed to come on full-time to run the ministry's new bookstore. You can pray for our family and our ministry.

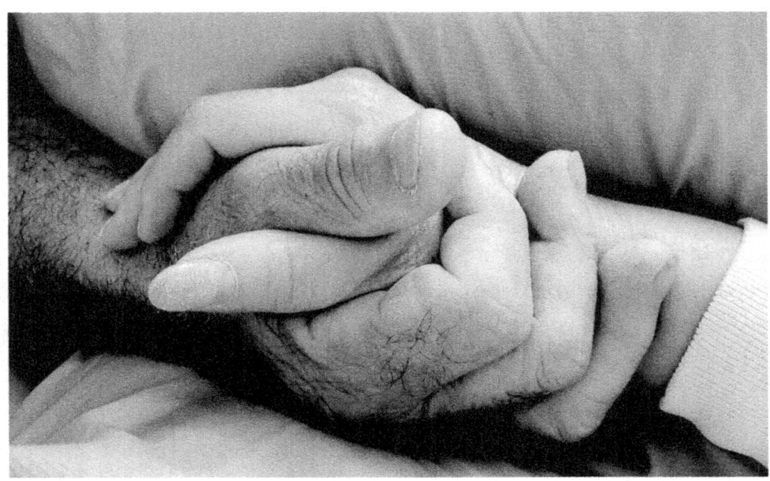

A Servant of God

Ashley had a real ministry for women who came to church without their husbands. He wouldn't always share even with me when he would go visit, but he had this thing of going to visit men who didn't go to church with their wives. His thing wasn't to get them to go to church but to befriend them. When men don't go to church, a lot of times, it's because of misconceptions about church. He wanted them to know there's normal guys at church. So, if he was in an area with his truck, he would stop and go visit. I found out some of those stories even at the funeral when people would come up to me and say you don't know how much that meant.

Some of the guys ended up in church; some never did, but he never stopped visiting them. I don't know where that came from except when the one who got saves was the only one in his family. His stepmom's parents went to church, but his dad and stepmom didn't. His dad got baptized the same day Ashley did and came up out of the water whooping and hollering like he was a Pentecostal, but after our wedding until his Dad died, he never entered church again.

Ashley was never worried about how a person that he visited was living at the time. He said some churches had it backwards. We're supposed to be fishers of men, but "They wanna clean 'em before they catch 'em. And cleaning is a process. That's God's job." So many churches want to be sure everything is right in a person's life before they are ready to let them into church. What God chooses to take out of their life, that's what God wants them to let go of first. That's God's job and the Holy Spirit's. We see the outside; God sees the inside.

My husband preached for our church on July 18, got sick in August, and passed in September. He preached on something people don't often preach on, "The Road to the Cross," the torture and all the things Christ went through. Less than a month, later his body is ravaged by this illness. He went septic with COVID pneumonia. It was just so striking that he had preached that sermon, and then so much suffering and pain happened to him.

Ashley was very tender-hearted. He could tear up easier than I could. When they put him on the ventilator, the first thing I missed was hearing his voice. That really hit me really, really hard—for him to go silent and not be able to do anything those last six days. I took pictures of us holding hands, and Ashley enjoyed reading all the messages and texts that came in. People would put their prayers on WhatsApp, and I would play them for him. He would listen to them over and over. That's what lifted him up and kept him fighting.

> **We're supposed to be fishers of men, but "They wanna clean 'em before they catch 'em. And cleaning is a process. That's God's job."**

Miracles for a New Widow

After Ashley died, my son Luke asked if he could use my husband's lunch box, and when he opened it, he found some of Ashley's things were still in it. There were those little rags for cleaning your glasses and a little square Precious Feet card with ten-week-old baby footprints on it. That was something Ashley always had with him. He always had them tucked away somewhere, usually in his shirt pocket, and when he'd meet a pregnant woman, he'd ask how far along they were, then show them the footprints. He'd say something like, "In two more weeks your baby's feet will be this size," or "Five weeks ago, your baby's feet were this size. They're a little bigger now." He never assumed that just because a woman was married that it was a wanted pregnancy, but he would tell them, "I want to give this to you because I want to thank you for choosing life and that precious child God is growing in your womb."

This is what gave my husband and me so much comfort when he was in the hospital dying. We kept saying God knew before he was knitted together in his mother's womb when he was going to leave this world, and he knew every step of his path Ps. 139:13-18 (NIV).

One thing I can see God put in place even before Ashley got sick is the women's Bible study I joined. A friend started it in March, and since Ashley had gotten his job back and I could count on him being at work, I was able to go. Seven months later, he passed. And I can say God put that Bible study in place wih the exact five people God needed me to have in my life at that time. Now we get together at my house once a month, play games, visit, laugh, and just have a good time.

People already ask me if I will marry again. All I can say is: If I'm ever going to be with somebody else, it's only because God's brought him to my door. I've got too much to keep me busy. The Lord's got me doing what I need to do.

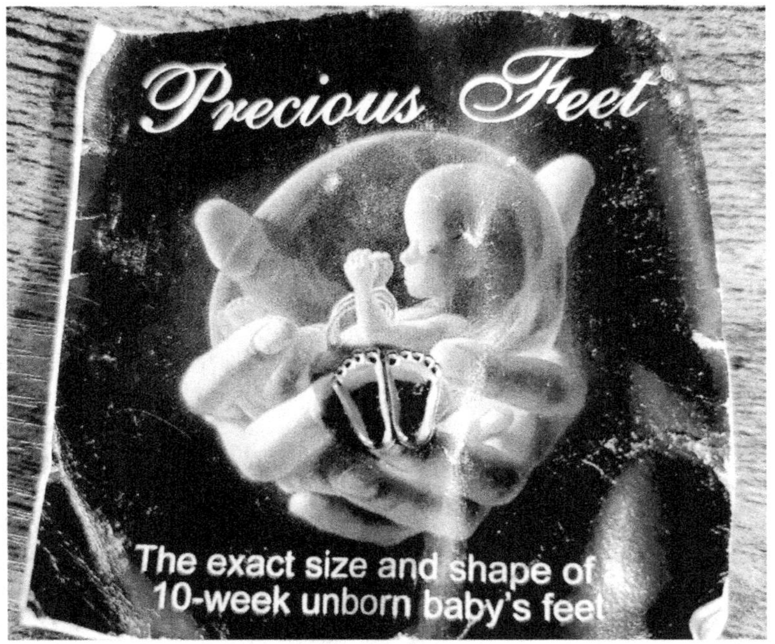
Precious Feet
The exact size and shape of a
10-week unborn baby's feet

WHAT WE DO AND WHY

Our Purpose

The purpose of Crossing All Borders Ministry is to share the Gospel of Jesus Christ. Our entire salvation is based on a relationship with a holy and living God. God created us in three parts that make one whole person. We're physically, mentally, and spiritually made, and when you're helping someone, and you don't address all parts, then you don't really help them. Just like that missionary who played handball with my dad for two consecutive years before he led my dad to the Lord. Or like Jesus feeding the 5,000. In my husband's vernacular, their stomachs were gnawing at their backbones, and God knew if He didn't meet that physical need, they wouldn't be receptive to His spiritual message.

That's how we say our ministry works. What we ship are tools for Christian missions, things that Christian organizations can't get where they are that will enable them to do their job. And God blesses us with so much stuff that we're a conduit to get that stuff to people who need it.

Gracias
JESÚS
thank you
JESUS

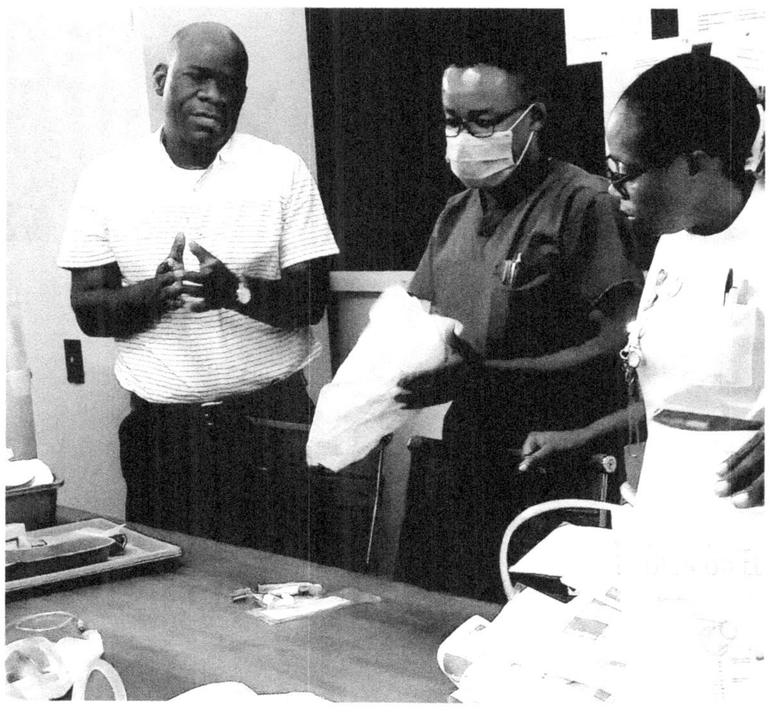

God Directs

Who would have imagined that a little girl who couldn't read until third grade, ridiculed in school because of her pigeon toes and eye patch and then permanently disabled in an accident, would be facilitating a ministry that brings Christians together across denominational lines to provide essential hard goods to Christian workers in 104 countries (so far!).

And yet, God had made me the kind of person who could patiently wait until He showed us His purpose for [millions of pounds of] seemingly random donated stuff. God gave me the contacts and skills I needed to organize international shipments that would reach their recipients behind Customs obstacles, across webs of bribery and corruption, in war zones, and in disasters. He taught me how to work with others—not just my family, who worked together to start this ministry, but with [hundreds] of volunteers God keeps sending.

I could not have picked a better journey for me if I had tried. If you gave any of us a catalog, none of us could choose a better journey than what God has chosen for us. We all look at others and say, "I couldn't do what they do." But God equipped them for their journey. He didn't equip you for their journey.

Sharing Jesus by Meeting Material Needs

The purpose of the ministry is simply to share the Gospel of Jesus Christ, plain and simple. When Christ fed the 5,000 in the Scriptures—they had a physical need. They were hungry. God met a tangible need before He met their spiritual need. That is what our product shipments do.

A lot of nonprofits are set up to do one thing and do it well. Whether it be helping the unemployed, pregnant women, homeless, drug addicted, disaster relief—you name it. There's a lot of different nonprofits out there. What they do is vital and awesome.

We help a lot of nonprofits in the community. We work a lot with Samaritan's Purse, the Baptist Men's Association, and the His Daily Bread Soup Kitchen that feeds about 200 people every Tuesday night a hot meal. With Love From Jesus is another partner. They bring products to us when they have overflow, and we send things to them when they have needs. And then we ship internationally—to ministries in 104 countries so far.

It's not a matter of who does what; it's a matter of just getting products to whoever needs them the best we can in order to share the Gospel of Jesus Christ. So, we partner with other nonprofits whose goal is to share the Gospel of Jesus Christ, build relationships with people, show the love of Christ, and then share the gospel with them. What we don't do is plain humanitarian aid that has nothing to do with making Jesus known. The reason we do what we do is to share the love of Jesus so people can be saved.

God Sends the Helpers – and the Tasks

Something I have never once done is go and look for anyone to act with. God has brought them to me because I'm too busy to go looking. Maybe someone sends me a note and asks me to call them. Or someone hears about us at a conference, and they call us. God has sent every volunteer to us and every ministry partner to us. Only God could connect us to 104 countries. That's just something I can't do. So, God continues to connect us with countries, missionaries, and individuals.

Sharing the Good News

Now, I've already mentioned that our whole reason for being is to share the Gospel. We put tracts and the Gospel of John in all of our packages. The other tool that we use a lot is a salvation doll. This doll has two faces. She's asleep on one side, and she's awake and smiling on the other side. People can use this to explain that when you do not know Christ, you're dead in your sins. But when you accept, you're a new creature, and you're alive in Christ. The doll also has colored beads that match the Gospel outline from *The Wordless Book* by Child Evangelism Fellowship:

- Black is for sin

  "For all have sinned and fall short of the glory of God" Rom. 3:23 (NIV).

- Red is for the blood shed on the cross

  "The blood of Jesus, his Son, purifies us from all sin" 1 John 1:7 (NIV)

- Blue is for the resurrection of Jesus Christ

Jesus said to her, "I am the resurrection and the life. The one who believes in me will live, even though they die" John 11:25 (NIV).

- White is He washes our sins white as snow

  "Though your sins are like scarlet, they shall be as white as snow" Isa. 1:18 (NIV).

- Green is growing in Christ once you accept Him

  "Grow in the grace and knowledge of our Lord and Savior Jesus Christ" 2 Pet. 3:18 (NIV).

- Yellow is heaven and the streets of gold

  "The great street of the city was of gold, as pure as transparent glass" Rev. 21:21 (NIV).

That book has been used for years and years and years to share the Gospel. Each doll goes out with cards explaining the message in whatever language they speak where they're being sent.

The Miracle of the Salvation Doll

The salvation dolls are made by Dolls on Mission out of Monroe, North Carolina by JoAnne Mucci who was a missionary for over forty years. When she came back to the States, she's like, "Lord, we can't serve on the foreign field anymore. What can I do to continue to share the Gospel?" and the Lord gave her this ministry. They make about $3,000 a month just for the salvation dolls.

So, when Campbell University medical students were going on one of their mission trips, I said: "Take twenty-five of these dolls, take twenty-five of these bags. I know it looks like a simple thing to take—just come back and tell me what happened."

Two weeks later Robert Rose comes walking into the warehouse and at first I didn't recognize him. But he says, "I need to speak to Joeth. I want to tell you what happened with those dolls. " And this is the story he tells me.

There's a man named Reese who's traveled on missions with Robert Rose and Dr. Joe Cappio for more than twenty-five years. These three have been on every single mission trip together. Reese is ninety-eight years old now. He travels in a wheelchair everywhere, and Reese's only job is to pray. He prays over the team, and he prays praise to God. That's all he does all day long and he's done that on these trips for all those years.

So, one day, he's looking out the doorway and notices that there's a girl feeling that salvation doll, and he recognizes that she's blind. Reese goes to somebody and asks about her story. And they said she's been blind since birth.

Reese laid hands on her and prayed for her, and God restored her sight at that moment. The first thing she ever saw was that doll. That's the first miracle. She got saved, and her entire family got saved. That's miracle number two.

God is still the God of miracles.

The miracles of the salvation dolls keep multiplying, too. On the most recent trip, there were more people saved through the dolls than the number of dolls they brought! That's because they told people who got saved to use the dolls to share the message of salvation. I'll tell you: When JoAnne Mucci gets to heaven, there's no telling how many people will be there because of her dolls.

The Miracle of the Message Cards

Here's another missions miracle. The Shepherd's Church was going on a mission trip to Kenya and wanted 200 dolls. But they needed the cards in Swahili. I said that was okay, because I knew that JoAnne at Dolls on Mission would be able to figure out how to do them.

So, I called, and I said, "JoAnne, I need some cards, but the mission group is leaving fairly quick." She said, "Joeth, before you tell me the language, let me tell you that God spoke to me last week and told me to make 200 cards. They're in an envelope on my desk on my counter here. I've already gone to the post office and gotten the postage on it. All I need is the address where to ship them." And then she said, "What was that language you need?" I said, "Swahili." She said, "Yeah, that's what God told me to make."

God is in everything.

Young Volunteers Come to Christ

We have lots of young people who volunteer at our warehouse. We have children from five high schools, including some football teams. And we share the Gospel with them.

We had a Bible study at my house for a while, and thanks to my son Luke's outreach to his friends, that study outgrew the house really fast. So, we moved it to church. These young people had never been in church; they didn't even know who Jonah was. We give them The Action Bible. It's got pictures like a comic book and tells them the Bible in story form, in chronological order, and it lists where the stories are in the Bible so they can look them up.

Over one weekend recently, we had nine baptisms and those young people were all excited. All their families came—all their parents and their siblings showed up. We set out seats for 112, and they were all full. I don't know many churches that have that excitement of the new believers. And not all churches disciple them anymore. Ever since then, we've had them serve both at church and the warehouse, and they love it. They ask, "What can we do to help?" They're not dressed up, they might have their ball caps on, but they just love to serve.

How a Forklift Witnessed to an Angel in Our Warehouse

God also uses us to share the Good News right in our own warehouse.

We had needed a forklift for quite a while. We had to borrow the forklift from the business behind us. They're very gracious to let us do that—the boss is fine with it, but some of the employees don't care for it, and they get a little frustrated with us. So, we'd been praying for a forklift. We did have one given to us, but it wouldn't hold a charge long enough to actually load a full container and there wasn't a cost-effective way to fix it. So, we kept praying for a forklift.

Well, we were doing another container for Ukraine, and Pastor Andriy from the Ukrainian church went back there to get the forklift and came to find out that the motor had seized. One of the employees, a guy named Angel, goes, "Why don't you get your Jesus to get her one?" So, Andriy came over to me, and he goes "Guess what? You're getting a forklift! Because God's not gonna be mocked. God hasn't given it yet, because He needs to give it now to show Himself to Angel. Now, let's see how God does it."

So that was on a Thursday. Andriy calls me to ask what other things we need and how much money we can spend. I told him he should call God's Pit Crew up in Danville, Virginia. They do fabulous disaster relief ministry, and they had donated forty-three generators before for us to ship. They also share donated resources in their area, kind of like we do. Andriy called them on Giving Tuesday to ask about a forklift, and Nathan Burnett, their director of ministry operations, goes, "Oh we've got one right here. You can come pick it up." So, in less than a week, from Thursday to Wednesday, we had a forklift.

Now, I didn't go back to Angel and say, "Look what we got!" No, God's gonna do what God wants to do in Angel's life. I don't need to act like that. But God's in everything that we do. We are so blessed to be able to serve Him. And just to see God's stories every day . . . I could talk to you from now until the Rapture, and we will not run out of stories that God has given us.

The Best Ways You Can Help

The two most important ways people help us are by volunteering and by letting us have durable goods that they no longer need or want.

It's incredible how much stuff we throw out in the US that can be used somewhere else. Mattresses, for example. Do you know that the college throws out mattresses every spring when the students go home? Through Amos Love at Beacon Ministries, we were able to arrange to pick up all the mattresses that Campbell University throws out in the spring. They're needed everywhere! So Campbell saves on their trash bill and gets a tax write-off, and we send them where they're needed.

Campbell's medical school has become a great source of medical supply donations, along with Wake Med [Health and Hospitals] and some others. There are so many things that get thrown away that can still be used.

Another good example is hospital beds. After a while, they're no good in the US because you can't get replacement parts for them, but in a country where they'll be sitting stationary in a room, that's not a problem.

We got a donation of bone stimulators from Embrace in Newport News, Virginia. They're made with a one-use lithium battery, so once they've been used that's it. But an engineer in Ukraine is trying to work out a way to rewire them so you can plug them in and use them over and over. Those are needed at a clinic somewhere in the world where they might not even imagine they exist!

Don't Just Give: Ask What's Needed, Give When Needed

One of the things we're able to do is to collect any new goods that people have too much of and hold it in our warehouse until God shows us someone who needs it. So, we make it easy for people to give whatever, whenever, and be sure it will go to someone who needs it and will use it for God's purposes.

But I'm gonna step on your toes here for a minute and talk about thoughtless giving. Every November and December, there's a great outpouring from our churches to homeless and lost people in our communities. Guess what? Those same people are around ten other months of the year, and they are in need those ten other months, too.

The outpouring in November and December is great. I'm not going to diminish what is going on in our community during those holiday months, but we tend to forget the people and the needs are out there ten other months.

We should be showing love to them every single month. I challenge every church to think about that and take action.

What Missionaries Need

Now, I'm going to tell you some things you might not know about living in another country, as a missionary that explains why we do the things we do.

There are lots of things we think are easy to get and cheap that aren't available at a reasonable price in other countries. I had a missionary that was in Honduras who needed a specific kind of lotion. It sells for $3.35 in Walmart here in the US and people would say, "Why don't you just send the money so they can go to Walmart and get it?"

But that lotion costs $45 a bottle in Honduras. I wouldn't be shipping something to them if they could get it in their country. It doesn't exist, or the cost is way too high. And even if they can get it there, I'll ship it if the cost of getting the item in the US plus the cost of shipping is lower than they can get it in their country. We make sure the price nets out right on everything we ship.

I want to tell you something else that most people don't know about living in other countries. Sometimes, a missionary will write home about "these wonderful berries I'm enjoying," and donors will stop supporting them because those berries are expensive in the US. "If they can afford that and I can't, why should I give them money?" the donors think.

What they're not thinking about is that those berries grow in the country where the missionary is working. That's why they're inexpensive there. The things my daughter enjoys at a low price where she lives in Costa Rica are totally different from the things I get at low prices in North Carolina. Just one example: grocery stores there have entire aisles of fifty-pound bags of rice, but here all I can find are tiny bags at Food Lion. So, trust your missionaries. When they say they need something, they do.

What Your Own Community Needs

You can even put this idea to work right at home. Do you know that living in a nursing home is a lot like living on the streets? Most people in nursing homes can't afford new underwear. They don't have money for a new pair of socks. They can't get an outfit when they need it. Most of the people in nursing homes don't have family to help them out.

If your church was to adopt just one nursing home, you could tell them to call anytime somebody in that home has a need, and you could make sure it's met. That would be huge! Because each person has different needs, and it can be kind of specialized. For example, some are able to handle a razor, but some can't. I know five people in wheelchairs who don't have any lap blankets, and they're cold all day. Nursing homes have a lot of diabetics. A lot of times a lot of food is brought in at Christmas time, and then they take two months trying to undo the damage done because generous people have jeopardized their health with foods they shouldn't eat.

So, I challenge you to consider that. If every church in every town were to help just one nursing home, trust me, there's enough churches to cover every single nursing home.

Let God Show What's Needed

I've been supporting missions for almost my whole life, but I made my first mission trip just a few years ago to Honduras. And what I learned on that trip was that I need to go to more places that I ship to because God was able to show me things they needed, but didn't know to ask for.

Here's the first thing God showed me. I was shipping into this one clinic. When I got there, the lady goes, "Oh, I share what you send with thirteen other clinics that are out underneath trees." You know, you go one hour in this direction, there's a tree, and there's a little clinic there. We had been shipping into this one clinic and they were sharing with thirteen other clinics that they had established all throughout the mountains. And I'm like, "Oh my goodness, we're not sending you anywhere close to what you need!"

And that's when I discovered that she didn't know what to ask for. So, I went into their storage room and I saw how they were set up, and it was just gut-wrenching to see how little they had and what basic items they didn't even know existed.

So, God has shown me that I need to go to more places and see more because I can see things. I have this memory that makes pictures I can look at later. That's how I know what's in every box and container I ship and how I know what's in our warehouse. I just look at the pictures in my memory.

In February 2023, I was blessed to sail on the Sea Hope into Jocmel, Haiti. We visited the hospital we were bringing things to, and I could see there were things needed that they hadn't requested. So, when I got back on the ship, I was laying in bed going, okay Lord, let me get back to the pictures in my head and let me look at each room and see what they're missing. And let me count the rooms. And as I looked through the rooms, I could see: they don't have this, they don't have that. So, then we were able to create a list of what needs to be on the next shipment to go in to try to fully equip His hospital—just with basic items. I mean, they were doing surgery without anesthesia because they didn't have an anesthesia machine. Oh my goodness!

The mission trips that God has sent me on, God has always had a purpose for me being there. I went on three mission trips in sixteen months, and I didn't plan any of them. God just opened the way. I went to Victoria, Honduras; Cartagena, Colombia; and Santo Domingo, Dominican Republic. And in all three of those trips, God planned it so I would learn how to better support the missions in each country.

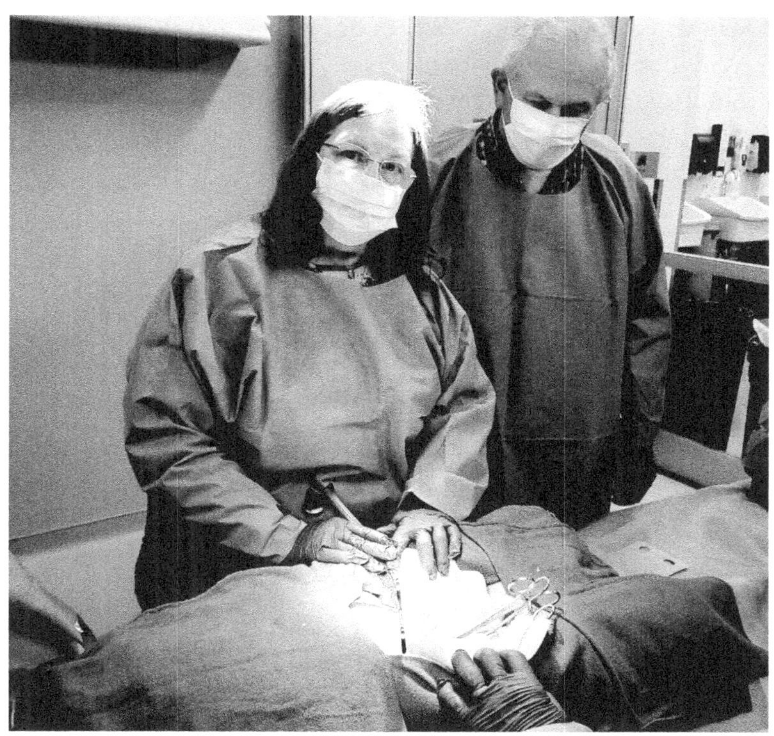

Don't Just Help: Be the Person God Made YOU

Every life is different. God has chosen your path just like God has chosen mine. Your path may be to come volunteer with us. You may come to us and learn about a ministry we help and realize that's where you need to be. But God's chosen your path. And everything in your life is a stepping stone for what He has ahead for you. God knew before you were knitted in your mother's womb. And He knows every step of your path. So, if you're not having a close relationship with Christ, and you're not sure where He wants to use you, trust me: you can be used by God.

Stop and think about the most important person to you in the world. You got that person in your mind? If that person were to call you today and ask you to do something, you would do it immediately, right? Why don't you do that with Jesus Christ? Why aren't we as excited to tell everyone about Jesus as we are to talk about that person?

That's why I consider it such a privilege to do what I do. The God of the universe could do everything without us, but He chooses to use us. We don't have a works salvation, but we have a salvation that works. It stands alone by itself; it's all of Christ. Still, Christ died and saved us from our sins and from this world so we could live in the way God chooses for us—not how the world pressures us to live. We don't work to have our faith; we work because God gave us faith.

I used to say I'm not smart enough to do this work, which is insulting to God. The organizational skills I have and my almost photographic memory—these are gifts from God to do the work of God. From the early years until now, it's God all over it. And your path also has God all over it. Just listen and watch and follow Him.

Our ministry is always grateful for volunteers. I try to work it out so we have about fifty volunteers at a time, whether that's from one group or four groups. But I also know that God has a specific plan for each person. When you come in to volunteer for us, you're not working for me. You're serving the Lord, and what you're doing is important because you're doing it for Christ.

He's made each person in such a way that they're prepared for exactly what God wants them to do. So when volunteers come to us, we give them opportunities to serve and also encourage them to get clear with God where God wants them to serve.

Sometimes that means they're only with us for a very short time.

There was one woman who came to volunteer who had an abortion when she was a teenager. She'd always wondered how God could use her after that. From volunteering with us, she learned about a local pregnancy crisis center where they needed volunteers who had her experience. When she went to volunteer there, it put her in a position to tell other women who have already had abortions that God can restore them the same as God has restored her.

Sometimes when people follow their God-given plan, we discover them as a partner, not a volunteer. That's how we connected with Sea Hope. Buddy Puryear was a retired Navy submarine captain, and it didn't take long before he got bored just sitting in the pew at church. "I can't do this anymore," he told his wife. So, they started praying, and God led them to use his skills as a ship captain to support missions.

They ended up carrying shipments to a Haitian church by way of the Puerto Rican church that had trained its pastor. Direct shipments from the US wouldn't go through, but shipments from another island could. So that made it possible for us to get medical supplies to Haiti.

Do What God Has Prepared You to Do

You need to do what God has prepared you to do. And not everyone will think the things God has gifted you with are gifts. My memory, for example. I have the kind of memory that if you ask me where anything is in my warehouse, I can tell you exactly where to go. That's a gift, and it's exactly what I need to run this ministry. But the doctors used to say it was because of trauma in my childhood. What they didn't know is that my dad had the same kind of memory. He was an orthodontist, and we would go walking in the mall at Crabtree and he'd see a person and tell me their name and what he'd treated them for in what year. His memory is amazing. He doesn't forget anything.

Same thing for emotional self-control. I don't have a lot of feelings, and that was a very good thing when I was pinned in that truck. Because of that, I could focus on my breathing, and talk to my dad, and hear from my angel without having a lot of fear run all over me. That's a gift, and it's exactly what my life has required.

Even Babies Can Volunteer!

A lot of nonprofits don't let children under the age of sixteen volunteer. I don't know why because we need to teach them when they're little, and kids love to help. My mom included me in everything—I started at four years old helping do this stuff.

My youngest volunteer was a little girl named Abby who started when she was just four months old. What did she do? Not much. We put a blanket in a shopping cart and put her in there. She mostly slept. But that mother had two older children in school and she needed to get out of her house. So, she could come in here with her baby and work and have adult conversations and be involved with other women. And from that, she went on to start a clothing closet in her own church. So now when people come to us, and they need clothes in the community, we send them over there.

We have another mother who brings in her daughter who is in a wheelchair. That was kind of neat because I was in my chair that day, and she's in a chair. But that mother is trying to help her daughter learn that she can be helpful, too. And she was praying for an electric wheelchair, and I get those all the time and get them fixed up, so I should be able to help her. We just got two children's sized chairs donated to be checked out to see if they can be fixed. Being in a wheelchair where somebody has to push you takes away your freedom because if you want to go anywhere, you have to ask somebody to help you.

You Don't Even Need to Be A Christian to Volunteer

We also don't require people to be a Christian to volunteer. One night when my mom was sewing some bags for us, she recruited my brother, who is not a regular churchgoer, to turn them inside out so she could add the handles. He did it for a while, then he's like, "I'm not doing this anymore. This is ridiculous."

So, he came up with an invention that turns them inside out for us. Now we tell him, "Look how God used you! You don't believe in Him, but He just used you."

God Might Surprise You

When you let the Lord use you any way He wants to, surprising things can happen. At least that's how it's been for me.

Me? Go on Mission Trips?

Now, I owe my salvation to missionaries. Our family was living on a military base in Japan when missionaries from Georgia, North Carolina, and Tennessee led me and my parents to salvation. So, I returned to the US in a first-generation Christian home. And from then on, my parents were very involved in missions. This was during the time when missionaries would stay on the field for five years, then they would come home for a year of furlough and needed a place to stay. My parents would get that housing set up, and my mother would work with the wives throughout the year to make sure they had whatever they needed to take back that was very expensive in the country where they served. She was a seamstress, and she sewed a lot of clothing for their children. I learned from childhood that we can support God's mission all over the world from our own homes.

I was not a believer in mission trips for a long time. I felt like short-term missions were the travel agency for American Christians. You'd hear people say, "Oh, I'm going on a mission trip." And it was all about what they were going to experience and see. Their hearts weren't where they should have been. But God still uses these trips in a mighty way to change a person's life. I understand that, even though the person that's changed is usually the person that went out, not the person that they went to see.

But my thing is, I'm always making sure I'm cost-effective in ministry. So, I'm thinking: okay, you have this church group going on a mission trip, and if you add up all the plane tickets and all the money spent, each person's trip is gonna cost $3,000. If you go with ten people, that's $30,000 right there. My mind was always thinking, "Instead of traveling there, why don't you take all of that money and send the money to the local pastor and say, 'Go, get what you need, hire people, give them jobs.'"

This same thought came up in our Perspectives class, too. American churches will take teams into places where there's need, and we'll build a church for them. But we'd do better, and they'd be better off, if we sent the money and let the local pastor hire local people to build their own church. Instead, they're looking on, and they're going "Why are they doing this? I don't have work because they're coming and doing it for us." It takes their sense of pride from them. Everybody wants to do for themselves. People don't want to take a handout. That's true in every culture.

What got me involved in missions travel was finding out that sometimes missions have needs they don't even know about.

Somebody anonymously blessed me by covering the cost for me to go on a trip to Honduras. We went to a medical clinic up in the mountains run by Mercy and Grace Ministries, a local-based ministry that we've been supplying for some time. Ricardo Venegas, one of the cofounders, called us into a room where a baby was dying. I didn't have any medical training, but he kept saying, "We need Joeth, they have a baby dying in this room."

Of course, after nineteen surgeries, I have gotten some medical knowledge. And so I could see what was the problem as soon as I got into the room. The baby needed a shot, and they only had one needle, the size you use for adults. I looked at them and said, "You need a butterfly needle," and they just looked at me like, "What's that?" They didn't know there are different size needles and a baby's veins are way too small for an adult needle.

So, they got the child headed to the hospital that day, and I got started visiting some of our missions to make sure they had what they need, not just what they know to ask for. And by invitation of Campbell University's medical school, I've just finished taking their mini-medical college program to help me know more.

Me? Take a Medical Course?

Studying medicine at a university is the last thing I'd expect of a person who got held back in school because she couldn't read! It just goes to show what God can do. I got to study at Campbell's mini-medical college in 2023. It's a short program, and I was there by invitation. I learned a lot! I also met the head of the medical school and thanked him personally for the hospital beds Campbell donated that were, at that moment, in a container on the way to Ukraine. I met a professor from Armenia who was going on a mission to Armenia with Campbell medical students. We provided supplies for that mission.

There's no telling what God will allow us to do or ask us to do if we're just open to how the Lord may lead.

If It's God's Will, It's God's Bill

I wouldn't have expected to ship thirty-six containers in a lifetime, much less to ship that many containers in just over a year. But that's what God planned, and that's what we've been able to ship just to Ukraine since the war there began.

We've had to stage the donation trucks coming in because so much is being prepared to go out. And this is from a ministry that didn't take any money at all for the first thirty-four years. We just did what God said to do. Because if it's God's will, it's God's bill.

God provides even the simplest-seeming things for us. I was praying recently for tape. Now I know that seems so simple, but let me tell you, tape is ridiculous. I paid $2 a roll before and it was twice the size. Now, it's like this little skimpy roll and they want six bucks. Well, that adds up really fast.

One day, someone volunteering in the warehouse asked me, "What's this pallet?" I said, "I don't know, I haven't had a chance to get to it." So someone else goes over there and looks into the first box and she goes, "Well, this box is tape." I said, "Are you kidding me?"

Well, not only was it tape, it was tape that fit our tape guns. Some of it was tape that doesn't need a tape gun. And I'm like, "Oh my goodness, that's two years of tape there for us."

So, we have learned that no matter how small, whatever your need is, God provides.

What's Next? God Knows!

We have miracles every single day in our warehouse. It's been mindblowing what God's been doing. As of today, God has used us to ship essential goods to 104 countries around the world, and we're still counting. We're preparing to open a Christian bookstore. We've been planning for several years and realized that COVID was one reason God had slowed that project. Now, we're aiming to open it in 2023.

Crossing All National Borders

We call our ministry Crossing All Borders, and we've crossed a lot of borders with our shipping. We've served Christian missions and churches on every continent of the world. We've been blessed that God has opened up for us the right kinds of shipping to get to each country. Every country requires shipping in a different size box, at a different price, to a different set of guidelines.

We don't use any US-based shipping companies because the costs are high, and you can't be sure the shipment will get there. But there are companies that ship to specific countries, usually owned by nationals, that the governments have given permission to ship into certain countries. When you use these companies, you get speedier customs clearance, and local couriers actually do the delivery. I can get boxes into refugee camps to people in Columbia who have fled there from Venezuela. We support 250 pastor's closets in just Venezuela, and we've shipped enough books to support twenty-five church-based schools.

Crossing All Denominational Borders

We are also crossing denominational borders by encouraging churches to work together in this ministry. We used to be based in the church that our family went to, but we'd never get all these volunteers if we were in just one church. When is the last time your church reached out to another church to say, "What can we do together so we can do more?" What God has showed us through this work is that a fire will burn really great if you get a lot of embers together, but if you put one ember off by itself it's going to go cold.

With the warehouse, all kinds of people come together to volunteer. People do things differently and churches do things differently. But when we work together across our denominations, we get more done. We avoid "forsaking the assembling of ourselves together" Heb. 10:25 (NIV) and instead build our faith and become better equipped to go out in the world.

It's Not Our story; It's God's Story That He Chose for Us

We started shipping a few crates for a ladies Sunday School class in 1984. We didn't know we were starting a ministry. But God knew He was starting a ministry in us. We started shipping the packages, and the ministry started growing. Where we are today is nothing I could have imagined or planned. You have to let God be at the helm.

I have flags hanging all over my warehouse from the countries we've shipped to. We don't have room for all 104! I was born again thanks to missionaries in Japan, and that's where God started my story—knowing what He had in store for me. The Scriptures are clear: The purpose God created us for is to bring honor and glory to Him. What better way than to live our journey that is His story through us?

We tell this story through daily posts on Facebook. I started this in 2018 after my kids made me my first Facebook account. I take pictures of whatever's happened in the warehouse, and people send me pictures of how what we've shipped is being used. The other day, some kids brought me some bikes, and they let me take a picture of them with the bikes to go on Facebook before I shipped the bikes off to Zambia. Then sometimes people get to see what they gave in use. So, one lady was clearing out clothes, and we sent those off, and then she got to see her dress on a girl in Ukraine. I think of this as accountability, but it also inspires people to donate. In the US, people have storage units full of stuff that someone else could use. When they see us shipping something they know they have, a lot of times they'll dig it out and give it to us.

> **Where we are today is nothing I could have imagined or planned. You have to let God be at the helm.**

When Will We Get Caught Up?

Our warehouse is full all the time. There's tons of stuff in there, and anybody can tell you that it's always full, even though stuff is going out as fast as it's coming in. Our amazing volunteers know when they come back, it's going to look entirely different because of what the next volunteers have done. That's how we can get done all the Lord's given us.

Bob Barker, whose company is our biggest single donor, used to come in and he'd say, "It looks the same every time I come in here. What are you doing with all this?" I'd tell him, "Bob, I sent fourteen pallets out yesterday and you sent twenty-eight back in behind that. I can't get caught up." And he'd shake his head and say, "Oh."

So trust me. The boxes that were in my warehouse three weeks ago are no longer there. It's constantly moving. We're blessed for that.

Somebody asked me recently, "So, when are we going to get caught up?"

And this is my new phrase:

"We will get caught up.
That will happen when we get caught up.
We should serve the Lord until we get caught up into heaven.
Until then, we should be serving the Lord."

What God Has Done Timeline

1984
Started mailing packages to missionaries for the Ladies Sunday School Class at Faith Bible Fellowship and worked out of the house.

1990
The space at home got too small, so we started using an empty Sunday School room at church.

1995
By now, we were using 3 rooms at church.

1999
- Got our first donation from Bob Barker Company.
- Helped fill containers to Angola, Zambia, and Romania.

2001
Shipped our first forty-foot container to Christian Missions Charitable Trust Orphanage in India.

2003
- Shipped our second container to India.
- Started picking up food from the food bank and distributing it to local families in need.

2012
Started using a much larger space in the back of a local church.

2017
Moved the ministry to be part of a warehouse space owned by Bob Barker (where we are currently).

2018
Became Crossing All Borders Ministry, an official 501(c)(3), nonprofit.

2019
- Was given an additional 2,000 square feet to use in the warehouse.
- Started receiving medical donations from Wake Med.

2020
- Bob Barker sold the warehouse to Jeff and Dan Hickman that own a welding business behind us. They graciously allowed us to stay.
- Too many items were being donated too quickly to distribute them so, we started an indoor yard sale to help fund the ministry.
- Bought a box truck

2022
We begin shipping forty-foot containers of essential supplies to Ukraine after war breaks out. By the middle of 2023, we've shipped thirty-six containers.

Countries Around the World that We Have Impacted with the Gospel

North and Central America

Belize

Canada

Costa Rica

El Salvador

Guatemala

Honduras

Mexico

Nicaragua

Panama

United States

Caribbean

Antigua and Barbuda

Bahamas

Barbados

Bermuda

Cuba

Dominican Republic

Haiti

Jamaica

Puerto Rico

Republic of Trinidad
and Tobago

St Kitts and Nevis

St Vincent and the Grenadines

South America

Argentina

Bolivia

Brazil

Chile

Colombia

Ecuador

Guyana

Peru

Suriname

Uruguay

Venezuela

Europe

Belarus

Belgium

Bulgaria

Czech Republic

Denmark

France

Italy

Latvia

Netherlands

Spain

Romania

Ukraine

Africa

Algeria

Angola

Burundi

Cote D'Ivoire

Democratic Republic of Congo

Egypt

Eritrea

Ghana

Ivory Coast

Kenya

Liberia

Libya

Madagascar

Morocco

Mozambique

Namibia

Nigeria

Republic of Congo

Rwanda

Senegal

Somalia

South Africa

Swaziland

Tanzania

Tunisia

Uganda

Zambia

Zimbabwe

Asia

Armenia

Bahrain

Cambodia

China

Indonesia

India

Iraq

Iran

Israel

Japan

Kuwait

Malaysia

Maldives

Myanmar

Nepal

Oman

Pakistan

Philippines

Qatar

Russia

Saudi Arabia

Singapore

South Korea

Sri Lanka

Taipei

Taiwan

Thailand

United Arab Emirates

Reference

[1]The course "Perspectives on the World Christian Movement" aims to help every Christian believer identify the role and opportunities God has given them to fulfill God's purposes among all the peoples of the world. It has been taught since 1974, when it was created by what was then called the US Center for World Missions.

OPPORTUNITIES TO GIVE & VOLUNTEER

"For God so loved the world that he gave his one and only Son, that whoever believes in him shall not perish but have eternal life."
John 3:16 (NIV)

WE DONATE TO:

- LOCAL FAMILIES
- LOCAL CHURCHES
- DRUG REHAB & ADDICTION FACILITIES
- PREGNANCY CRISIS FACILITIES
- HOMELESS SHELTERS
- SOUP KITCHENS
- INTERNATIONAL MINISTRIES
- DISASTER RELIEF
- MEDICAL SUPPLIES

JOETH STRICKLAND
910-890-7201

donations@crossingallbordersministry.com

www.crossingallbordersministry.com

Mailing: P.O. Box 132, Lillington, NC 27546

Made in the USA
Columbia, SC
15 December 2023

28600868R00063